101 Music Games
for Children

101
MUSIC GAMES
FOR CHILDREN

Fun and Learning
wlth Rhythm and Song

Jerry Storms

translated by Anne Griffiths

a Hunter House SmartFun book

Library of Congress Cataloging-in-Publication Data

Storms, Ger.
[Muzikaal spelenboek. English]
101 music games : fun and learning with rhythms and songs / Jerry Storms.
— 1st ed.
p. cm.
Translation of: Muzikaal spelenboek.
Includes index.
ISBN 0-89793-165-3 (spiral bdg.) : $12.95
ISBN 0-89793-164-5 (soft cover) : $9.95
1. Games with music. 2. Music—Instruction and study—Juvenile.
I. Title. II. Title: One-hundred-one music games.
MT948.S8413 1994
781.4'2—dc20   94–11810
CIP   MN

Project Manager: Lisa Lee   Production Manager: Paul J. Frindt
Cover design: Jil Weil Graphic Design   Book Design: *Qalagraphia*
Illustrations: Cecilia Hurd   Translated by: Anne Griffiths
Editors: Deborah Grandinetti, Rosemary Wallner, K.S. Rana
Sales & Marketing: Corrine M. Sahli   Publicity & Promotion: Darcy Cohan
Customer Support: Sharon R. A. Olson, Sam Brewer
Order Fulfillment: A & A Quality Shipping Services
Administration: María Jesús Aguiló
Publisher: Kiran S. Rana
Typeset in Charter by 847 Communications, Alameda CA
Printed and bound by Data Reproductions Corporation, Rochester Hills MI
Manufactured in the United States of America

9   8   06   First edition

Ordering Information

Trade bookstores and wholesalers in the U.S. and Canada, please contact

Publishers Group West
4065 Hollis, Box 8843
Emeryville CA 94608
Telephone 1-800-788-3123 or (510) 658-3453
Fax (510) 658 1834

Special sales

Hunter House books are available at special discounts when
purchased in bulk for sales promotions, premiums, or fundraising.
For details, please contact

Special Sales Department
Hunter House Inc.
P.O. Box 2914
Alameda CA 94501–0914
Telephone (510) 865-5282
Fax (510) 865-4295

College textbooks/course adoption orders

Please contact Hunter House at the address and phone number
above.

Orders by individuals or organizations

Hunter House books are available through most bookstores or can
be ordered directly from the publisher by calling toll-free:

1-800-266-5592

Contents

A detailed list of games with appropriate age levels starts on the next page.

List of Games

List of Games, continued

List of Games, continued

List of Games, continued

List of Games, continued

Preface

In opening this book you are entering relatively unexplored territory. Not much practical material exists on how to use music and sound games in a setting that is educational yet fun. This book will give you a hundred and one—actually a hundred and *two*—ways to explore this territory. It will also give you the tools to create musical games of your own for family, friends, or students.

Using music as an inspiration for games is not new; people have been doing it for centuries. Music energizes games and gives them added dimensions of fun and imagination. Some composers have even used games to inspire their music. We know, for example, that Mozart composed musical scores with the help of dice when he wanted to save his creative energy. More recently, the American composer John Cage used the *I Ching*, the Chinese oracle, to determine the course of a composition.

But you don't have to be a Mozart or a John Cage to make music fun. The playful, creative potential of musical expression is something *everyone* can enjoy and share. There is nothing more natural, for example, than a parent calming an infant with a lullaby or singing cheerful nonsense songs to make a young child laugh.

Sometimes, as the child gets older, the songs become call-and-response games. These improvisations are expressions of love as well as a form of play; they encourage bonding between parent and child. Later the child may form ties with peers through musical games such as "Ring Around the Rosy" and "Musical Chairs."

For a while, music played a broad role in education, one that went beyond the traditional curricula of music theory and composition, voice development, or learning a musical instrument. However, with increasingly tightened budgets and changing opinions about the role of education in developing the whole person, music just doesn't find a place in most U.S. schools anymore. Which makes this book even more important.

I have been particularly fascinated by the use of music in games designed to encourage positive and harmonious interactions within a group and confident self-expression by group members.

Please realize that these games are not meant to provide *musical instruction*. They are, however, an excellent preparation for musical education because they foster relaxed attitudes and open-mindedness about music, and allow participants to experience firsthand the pleasures of playing with music.

Among those who have helped to pioneer the use of musical games for instructional purposes are Murray Schafer, Brian Dennis, and John Paynter. In my own work I was inspired by Ad Heerkens, a teacher from the Netherlands who has used music and sound games to encourage creativity in children and adults. He has truly advanced understanding of the potential of musical expression. The widespread positive response to his work encouraged me to set up a similar method of using music games in high school classes. I went on to use the games in a number of settings where I came into contact with people of all ages. From observations of what worked and what didn't—gathered over twenty years—I revised and improved the games. The results are in this book.

I would appreciate your reaction to the games and the presentation of this material. Please use the evaluation form at the back of the book to send your comments, new ideas, and any suggestions for improvement to me, care of the publisher.

I wish you much pleasure in your musical play.

Jerry Storms
February 1995

Introduction

The Benefits of Play

People mean quite different things when they talk about "the sublime playing of a pianist," for example, and "playing a game of table tennis." The games of music and sound in this book fall into the latter category. The emphasis is on play, not on performance. And although the games are played according to certain rules, the quality and nature of the *process* of the game is largely determined by the character and ability of the participants.

Generally, each participant in a game has two levels of experience: the outer experience of the game itself, and the inner experience of how and what he or she feels as the game progresses. If you, as the observer or group leader, focus only on the outer game, you may not find it very interesting unless some exciting element is added, such as competition. If you look no further than that, however, you will miss most of what is really happening. These games provide the participants with some very tangible—if not entirely visible—benefits.

For example, these games make it possible to:

- **Take a break from daily routine.** When we really get involved in a game, daily realities fade away. Worries are temporarily put aside. Only when the game is over does the outside world intrude again.

- **Become totally absorbed in an activity.** Games can fascinate and completely engross us—sometimes to the point of addiction. Few other activities draw us in as completely as games do.

- **Think, feel, and act in an integrated way.** Few day-to-day situations require us to think, feel, and act simultaneously. Most jobs or studying require more thinking than feeling or acting. When we walk, exercise, or do routine chores, we tend not to engage our intellect or emotions. And emotions tend to come into play, for many of us, during passive activities, such as watching movies or sports, or listening to music. Successful play, however, usually requires involvement and coordination of all our faculties: intellect, emotions, and motor skills. This is what makes games so rewarding.

The Purpose of this Book

Having fun is certainly an inspiration for these games. But because I would like this book to be more than a simple collection of games, I'd like to emphasize what *else* goes on in them besides fun. These music games are really tools for learning. The following pages explain in more detail the aims of the games, the group dynamics at work, and what you need to get started. There is also information to help you decide which games to choose for different settings and how to put your own ideas into action by creating new and original games suited to your needs.

The relationship between music games and music training

There are certain specific reasons for using music and sound as the basis of these games, all of which enhance knowledge and appreciation of music, including:

1. Playing with music and sound gives participants the confidence to use basic musical concepts and materials. The games put them in touch with elementary ideas such as high and low notes, soft and loud sounds, slow and fast tempos.

2. Children who play these games regularly become comfortable and familiar with musical elements. Children also come into contact with their own musical potential in a way that is spontaneous and nonjudgmental.

3. Participants in the games get to play with different instruments and get hands-on experience making music. This can be so much fun that they are often inspired to pursue further musical training.

4. Playing with music also helps children overcome fears about making music. It combats ideas such as "I'm not musical because I can't play an instrument."

When you are leading these games, take special care to remember that an informal approach to the games is essential. This helps to create the climate of trust and comfort necessary for each child to be herself or himself and express that self fully and spontaneously. Until the group achieves that feeling of trust and until it is clear that the children are enjoying the activity, it is too early to provide more structured musical training. When children have reached a point of comfortable and active expression in the games, you should watch for signs that show they need or want further training. Then you can provide suggestions or direct them to other sources.

Why the emphasis is on social games

Next to dance, music is the most social of the arts. These games are designed to bring participants together in a way that encourages children's overall learning and creativity and develops the following key skills:

- effective listening
- increased concentration
- creative self-expression within a group
- social behavior that is considerate of others

Who Should Use this Book

This book is for parents who have a group of children in their house or yard who need entertaining, whether it's party time, vacation time, or family time; music and other teachers, pre-school or kindergarten through high school; camp counselors involved with any age group at camp; cubscout and scout leaders; day care centers; church groups; and everyone else who leads children in play and is looking for new ways to amuse and educate them.

None of these games calls for dividing the group into those who are unskilled and those who are musically gifted. Nor do they require that the children know how to play musical instruments.

You, the group leader, will not need any musical experience or expertise either. Consider yourself musical enough to lead these games if you recognize the theme from your favorite TV show, or if you can hum a tune or enjoy listening to music on the radio. All you need is enthusiasm, commitment, adaptability, the ability to work with groups of children of all sizes and ages, and the openness to share their enjoyment of the music and sounds they create.

The Games and Their Objectives

The games in this book are organized into three groups: those that develop *personal* skills, those that develop *social* skills, and those that develop *creative* skills. Within each of these groups I have identified three different styles of games, making a total of nine categories. Each game is clearly marked to indicate the most suitable age group, the time required, the supplies needed, and the ideal group size. Many of these games can be played indoors or outdoors, so you can choose a game that suits the weather.

The three groups are discussed in more detail below.

The first group, **games that develop personal skills,** focuses on the individual and includes:

- listening games

- concentration games

- musical quizzes

The ability to listen and concentrate is considered essential in all learning processes. Education in particular makes considerable demands on these abilities, but they are increasingly threatened in these times. We find ourselves surrounded by more and more noise and ambient sound, which makes focused listening more difficult. At the same time, the number of impressions we receive simultaneously and are expected to digest makes growing demands on our powers of concentration. The games in this category help to build directed and selective listening skills and heighten the ability to concentrate in the face of distractions. The musical quizzes encourage children to develop their memories, remain aware, and pay attention.

The **games that develop social skills**—learning to get along with each other—help to strengthen and increase group unity and communication. They can also speed up the acceptance of an individual into the group. They include:

- games for getting to know each other

- interaction games

- trust games

Depending on your objectives, you can use these games to help group members learn about each other, loosen up, reduce nervousness, warm up for a more difficult exercise, or build confidence in themselves and each other. These games can also help members of the group become better at considering other people's feelings and taking risks.

Through a careful choice of the right activities these games can help a new class or play group quickly begin to function as a cooperative, close-knit unit, rather than as a collection of individuals who just happened to come together. They can also be used for groups—such as families—that have known each other for a while but have not played together much, if at all.

The third group, **games that develop creative skills,** can help to increase participants' confidence in their creative abilities. They include:

- games for self-expression and improvisation

- seeking and guessing games

- musical board games

Everyone is creative in some way, but it can be difficult to bring out this creativity. This is especially true in education, where activities that develop cognitive skills are given more attention than those that foster creativity. These games are also important in a larger, more long-term context. Only when people experience their own free-flowing creativity are they able to at least recognize noncreative work and maybe even liberate themselves from it. This has considerable implications for modern society, which increasingly demands people who are flexible and inventive. Those who have learned to think and respond creatively have a better chance of keeping pace with change and becoming productive, fulfilled adults.

In each game's description, there is more discussion of its particular features and benefits. As you work with these games, you will see that each game has many possible variations. You or your players will often be able to create better and more effective versions of the games. Don't hesitate to adapt, shorten, or extend them according to the needs and wishes of the group.
You will also see that categorizing the games is quite a subjective process. Many of the games overlap, and there are similarities in structure as well as in function. Certain games contribute to the achievement of several objectives, and for all of them the result depends a great deal on the attitude toward the game and the aspect on which the leader chooses to focus.

Icons Used with the Games

To help you find games suitable for a particular occasion and group all the games are coded with symbols called icons. These icons tell you at a glance four things about the game:

the appropriate age group

the amount of time needed

the size of group needed

required instruments or props

These are explained in more detail below and a full listing of the icons is given on page 12.

Suitability in terms of age. There is a difference between games for young children, older children, teenagers, and all ages.

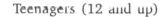

Young children (up to age 7)

Older children (ages 8 through 12)

Teenagers (12 and up)

All ages

How long the game takes. The games are divided into those that take 5 to 10 minutes or less, those that take up to 15 minutes, those that go on for 30 minutes or more, and those in which the time depends on the group's size.

Less than 5 minutes

Up to 15 minutes

30 minutes or more

Time depends upon group size

Whether you need a large group, small group, or a specific number of players. For example, small groups are those with fewer than ten participants. Some games require an even number of players, or a number that is a multiple of three or four.

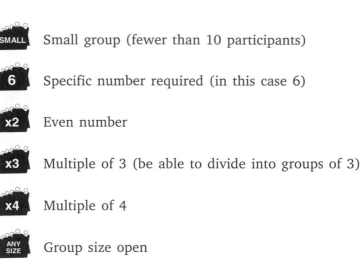

SMALL   Small group (fewer than 10 participants)

6   Specific number required (in this case 6)

x2   Even number

x3   Multiple of 3 (be able to divide into groups of 3)

x4   Multiple of 4

ANY SIZE   Group size open

Select a game suitable for the numbers in your group.

Whether you need instruments or props. Some of the games make use of voice alone. Others require specific instruments for each player, or two of each instrument so players can work in pairs. Other games call for blindfolds, record players, etc. The requirements are listed for each game, and the icon gives you a quick way to check.

    Instruments needed

    Props needed

Considerations for the Leader

There is more to being a games leader than just explaining the game. You need to be organizer and observer, coach and referee.

As the **organizer,** you are responsible for providing the necessary supplies and equipment and organizing the room or space for the game. You can lose momentum if the group has to set up the room and hunt for supplies.

You should also be able to clearly explain the **rules or order of play,** which requires preparation on your part. Make sure you understand the rules, in case you have to act as referee. How will you respond if someone bends a rule but doesn't quite break it? The better prepared you are to handle any situation that comes up, the smoother the game will run.

A **positive attitude** is also important. As the leader you must have faith in the effect of the game on the group and be convinced of the value and potential success of what you are doing. You may also need to be an **initiator.** A game doesn't always run on its own, and you may need to give it a push to get it going. Your enthusiasm can help to get things off to a good start.

Once the game has started, **observe** it keenly but discreetly. Remember that you can't foresee everything that might happen. Close observation will allow you to decide whether to interfere, either to remind participants about the rules or the care of instruments and supplies, or for some other reason.

Think about the best way to **set up the groups** for different games. Should the same people always sit next to each other? In competitive games, are the numbers well balanced?

Above all, watch and remember the behavior and reactions of the participants during the game so that you can **provide feedback** at the end.

As group leader, should you take part in the game? There are two ways to look at this. The advantage of taking part is that the group has a chance to experience you as a group member, which can strengthen your relationship with them. However, you might lose your overall view of the game and the group, which will limit your ability to give feedback. This is less of a problem in small groups, where the overall picture is easier to grasp. If you decide to join in a game, choose to do so in small groups rather than larger ones.

Which games to choose

A key aspect of your role as leader is to *choose* the right game for your group, one that takes into consideration the group's age, skill level, ability to concentrate, attention span, and the space and resources available to you.

First, think about which skills you want your group to

learn—personal, social, or creative—and select a game from one of those three groups.

Next, consider the game and the mental demands it will make on the group. Most games are constructed in two ways: open and closed. **Closed games** are fixed, unchangeable, and the rules may not be altered. This type of game is well suited to children who do best when given a solid framework. **Open games** have fewer rules and are more flexible. These games allow for more individual contribution, which can be difficult for some children.

In general, it is best to follow this principle: the more developed the group, the more open you can be in your choice of the game; the less developed the group, the more structured you need to be in your relationship with them and in your presentation and choice of games.

Finally, do you have the necessary supplies on hand? If you want a minimum of fuss, then consider those games that require no supplies. On the other hand, if you want to put together a musical games tool-kit, be on the lookout for: a CD or cassette player, blindfolds, and small portable instruments such as bongos or drums, tambourines, cymbals, rattles, recorders, xylophones, penny whistles, guitars, and so on.

If none of these is available, you can make your own noisemakers, using inexpensive materials. Working with real instruments is stimulating but not absolutely necessary, and some ideas for homemade instruments are given on page *14.

Here are some final considerations when selecting a game:

1. Level of difficulty. Remember, not all games are suitable for all age groups. Think about whether a particular game is suitable for your group, or so difficult it will create more frustration than enjoyment. For example, if you choose a game that requires serious concentration by a group of giggly young children, everyone will feel frustrated, at least at the outset. Games that require plenty of action are more suitable for this age group.

2. Space. Some games require a place where you won't be disturbed. If this is not available, avoid the trust and concentration games.

3. Length of play. I have given approximate times for each game. Remember, on the whole it is better for a game to be too short than too long.

4. Wise use of instruments. If you are using musical instruments you should be able to demonstrate how to play them. Impress upon the group the importance of taking good care of instruments. Let them know how much the instruments cost or explain the effort you put into making them. Hand out the instruments after you have finished your explanation.

5. Discipline. During the game, you should be a cheerleader, encouraging everyone to express themselves freely through the music. If the game shows signs of getting out of control, however, you should interrupt it firmly. A leader who cannot keep control will lose the respect and interest of the participants.

6. Competition. This can be an important motivating factor, especially for children who otherwise need encouragement. Present the games so that *each* child, regardless of his or her musical or other abilities, has a chance to win. You don't have to score a music board game or quiz based on musical knowledge. Instead, reward qualities such as humor, fantasy, cooperation, and so on. Although competition can give a boost to the group's ingenuity, imagination, and originality, there should be no judging of musical talents.

Conclusion

Clearly, there is more than just fun to be gained from the games.

I have created a simple comparison chart to clarify the games' objectives. The music and sound games in this book:

Are intended	*Are not intended*
to create an informal and trusting atmosphere in a group	to create a situation where the group focus is on winning and losing

to create and stimulate group processes through which creative, social, and personal skills can be developed	to teach a group any one specific skill
to take a regular place within the music lesson as preparation for musical education	to take the place of ordinary music lessons
to show what might be possible at school in other subjects	to compensate for the lack of creativity in other school subjects and with other materials
for use in adapted form in remedial situations	as an alternative form of music therapy

Key to the Icons Used in the Games

Age

 Young children (up to age 7)

 Older children (ages 8 through 12)

Teenagers (12 and up)

 All ages

Time

Less than 5 minutes

Up to 15 minutes

30 minutes or more

 Time depends upon group size

Group size

 Small group (fewer than 10 participants)

 Specific number (in this case 6)

 Even number

 Multiples of 3

 Multiples of 4

 Group size open

Props

Instruments needed

Props needed

If neither symbol is shown, no instruments or props are needed.

Suggestions for Homemade Musical Instruments

Coffee can with two plastic lids and a handful or dried beans or rice grains (rattle)

Kitchen pot or cookie sheet and a wooden spoon (percussion)

Cardboard box and wooden spoon (drum)

Dried gourds (rattles)

Empty paper towel rolls (trumpets). These can be decorated to look more fun.

Baby toys, with bells or rattles

Castanets, made from two wooden spoons with most of the handles cut off. Make two holes in what is left of the handles and tie together with string, then paint patterns on them.

Glasses or glass bottles, filled to different levels with water (xylophone)

Empty gallon jugs or large plastic bottles, cut in half and covered with plastic, with a few dried beans or rice grains inside (shaker). These can be painted or decorated.

Jingle bells, sewn on elastic. The ends can be sewn together to make a band so they can be worn on a wrist or ankle.

Games that Develop Personal Skills

Listening Games

These games teach attentive listening and require participants to react to various sounds, either by imitating them, copying their rhythm, etc. There is a difference between games that teach listening and those that teach concentration, although there is also some overlap between the two. In a typical listening game, superficial listening may be sufficient whereas concentration games require more focused listening. Listening games are easier for children who find it hard to concentrate, and it is often better to use these as a first step. Move on to concentration games only after your play group has mastered listening games.

Chief Characteristics of Listening Games

- The chief objectives are comparing and recognizing sounds.

- They draw on memory and intelligence, and exercise the participant's ability to respond quickly and improvise.

- They often use blindfolds, since attention to sounds is much easier with eyes closed.

- Most of the games are intended for young children.

1

Tracking Down

Requires: A different instrument for each person; a blindfold

Directions: Seat group members in a circle and give each one an instrument. Blindfold one child and place him in the center. Then name an instrument, such as a bongo drum. Motion to everyone to start playing at the same time. The child wearing the blindfold has to listen carefully and try to find out where the named instrument is, then get up and get a hold of it. Until he does, group members should keep playing. When he has the instrument in his hands, another child takes a turn in the center.

Note: Make sure everyone in the group knows the names of all of the instruments in use.

Variation 1: If you do not have enough musical instruments, have everyone imitate the sound of different instruments. The person wearing the blindfold must track down one particular instrument and touch the child.

Variation 2: Have everyone make a vocal sound. The child wearing the blindfold tries to track down and touch one particular child by recognizing his or her voice.

2

Which Instrument Is Missing?

Requires: A different instrument for each person

Seat group members in a circle. Each person but one takes a different instrument. The person without an instrument listens carefully while the others take turns playing something, so that each makes a recognizable sound.

Seat the child without an instrument with her back to the group and have her close her eyes. Once she cannot see you, point to an instrument that will *not* be played. Have the others start playing at the same time. The listener has to try to tell which instrument is not joining in.

Note: Make sure group members know the names and recognize the sounds of all the instruments. You can also include any large instrument, such as a piano, organ, or drum, that is available.

3

Imitation Game

Requires: Two instruments of each kind

Divide the group in two and have the two subgroups sit with their backs to each other. Place an identical selection of instruments in front of both groups. When you signal, someone from the first group should play something on any one of the instruments. The second group must decide, from the sound alone, which instrument is being used and then someone from that group must play something on the same instrument that is in front of them. If their choice is correct, the second group wins a point.

After this, have the groups change roles. Agree in advance that the game will be stopped after a certain number of rounds have been played or a certain number of points have been scored.

Variation 1: Play the instrument in an unusual way, so the sound is harder to identify.

Variation 2: Make the game more difficult by having the second group imitate the rhythm used by the first group.

4

Name Game

Requires: An instrument for each person

Have each group member take an instrument and sit in a circle. Each will take a turn saying his or her first name and surname and playing the rhythm of their names on their instrument. Mary Roberts would be

and Wee Willie Winkie would be

Every time someone says his name and plays his rhythm, have the whole group repeat the rhythm a few times. After you complete one round, have someone play on his instrument the rhythm of another person. As soon as that person recognizes it as her rhythm, she should react by playing the rhythm of someone else's name, who in turn reacts by playing the rhythm of another person's name, and so on.

Note: Some children may require a little help in the beginning to get the right rhythm for their name.

5

Changing Chairs

Requires: A blindfold

Seat group members in a compact circle. Blindfold one person and place her in the middle of the circle. Give each person around the circle a number, but don't let the person who is wearing the blindfold know who has what number. Ask the person wearing the blindfold to call out two numbers. The two people who have those numbers try to change places as quietly as possible. Using the sound as her cue, the person wearing the blindfold tries to tag one of them. While they are changing places, the two people are not allowed to run back to their own place. Once they sit down, it is too late to tag them. When the person in the blindfold succeeds in tagging someone, they swap roles.

6

How Many People Behind Me?

Requires: A blindfold

Have the group members stand in a circle. Blindfold one child and have him stand in the middle. When you signal, several children should move, one by one, and stand behind the person wearing the blindfold. Make it clear that the other group members need to be as quiet as possible. The person wearing the blindfold must listen carefully and guess how many people are standing behind him. When he has guessed correctly, someone else gets to be blindfolded.

7

Guessing a Song

Divide the group into smaller subgroups or, in a small group, have the members play on their own. Clap, tap, or play the rhythm of a well-known song all the way through. At the end, the first group or individual to name the song correctly wins a point. Whoever has the most points after a certain number of rounds is the winner.

Variation: For older children, use this short game as part of a larger game, such as a quiz game or musical board game, a variation described in the last section of the book.

8

Where Am I?

Requires: A blindfold

Allow the group to look around and become familiar with the room. Then blindfold one person and lead her to a corner of the room. Everyone else can stand anywhere in the room, and should remain there. The person wearing the blindfold calls out the name of one of the participants, who makes a sound on a surface close by (such as the floor, a door or window, or a piece of furniture). After the participant has made the sound a few times, the person wearing the blindfold must figure out where he is standing. When she succeeds, someone else takes her place.

9

Musical Discussion

Requires: An instrument for each person

Seat group members in two rows facing each other. Each person should sit exactly opposite someone in the other row. Give everyone an instrument. Each person in the first row, by turns, plays something on his or her instrument and the person directly opposite imitates the sound as closely as possible. When everybody in the first group has played something, change roles.

Then have each person in the first row play something on his or her instrument while the person opposite *responds* to it, as if answering a question. Again, work through to the end of the row and change roles.

Now have two pairs join together, forming a group of four. One person in this group begins an improvisation on her instrument while the others listen. The idea is for her to "say" something using her instrument, to which any of the other

three may react. Then another member of the group reacts to the reaction, just as you might in a normal conversation.

After a few minutes, stop the "discussion" and ask the audience what they noticed. Did people in the group really listen to each other? Who spoke a lot and who spoke a little? Did the way of playing express something? After this talk, the next group of four can begin their musical discussion.

10

Who Is Singing the Loudest?

Requires: A blindfold

Have the children sit or stand in a circle. Blindfold one group member and put her in the middle. Have the whole group sing a song together, but ask each person to sing at a different volume. To do this, have everyone agree in advance—and in secret—who will sing very soft, soft, moderately loud, or very loud. One child must agree to sing the loudest of all.

The child wearing the blindfold listens and tries to name the child who is singing the loudest. Then she has to find that person and tap him. When she succeeds, blindfold the child who was singing the loudest and begin again.

11

Guessing Games

Sing a well-known song several times. Without making it too obvious, change something in the tune or lyrics. The first person to discover and correct the mistake wins a point.

Variation: Use this short game as part of a quiz or musical board game.

12

Night Patrol

Requires: A blindfold, or a space in which children can hide

Ask one person, who is to be the night patrol, to leave the room. Then give each remaining member of the group a number and have each think of an animal sound. No one is to know anyone else's number or sound. Instruct group members to hide.

Once everyone is hidden, ask the night patrol to come back in and call out a number. The person with that number must make his or her animal sound. If the night patrol correctly guesses the name of the animal, the child has to come out of hiding while the night patrol tries to catch him or her. If the night patrol makes a wrong guess, he has to try again and nobody need move.

Note: In a small room you could blindfold the night patrol so that there is no need to hide. Instead, have the children take up a fixed place in the room and stay there. The game can be even more exciting if it is played in the dark, in which case the night patrol would have to locate, rather than catch, the person in hiding.

13

Remembering Sounds

Requires: Objects in the room you can use to produce sounds

Ask group members to relax by lying on the floor or sitting in a chair and closing their eyes. Spend six minutes making sounds, using whatever you have at hand. You can tap on the heater, open and close the curtains, rattle the trash can, etc. Have everyone try to guess and write down what they think they have heard, preferably in the right order. When you are done, compare the results.

Note: This game develops good listening skills. This and similar exercises become more interesting the more often they are repeated, especially if you keep track of the group's results and progress.

14

Playing by Ear

Requires: An instrument for each person, two different instruments for the leader

Take two very different instruments, such as a bongo drum and xylophone, and keep them in an adjoining room, hidden from the group. Give each child in the group an instrument and tell them that they should only join in and play when you are playing *one* of the hidden instruments. For example, they should only join in when they hear you play the bongo, not when you play the xylophone.

Keep changing from one instrument to the other, faster and faster, staying out of sight of the children. This way, they can only use their ears to decide whether to play or not.

Variation 1: You can also have one of the children conduct this game.

Variation 2: Have one half of the group play along when you play one instrument, and the other half play when you play the other.

15

Freeze-Frame

Requires: A CD or cassette player or radio

Put on music that is lively but not too wild. Ask group members to move, run, or dance freely in time to the music. Stop the music suddenly. When you do, everyone must freeze in whatever position they are in. Make sure nobody moves for about 20 seconds, then begin the music again.

16

Musical Relay Race

Requires: A rhythm instrument for each subgroup, four sticks or flags, a large open space. Ideally, the size of the group should be a multiple of four.

Divide the players into groups of four and give the members of each group numbers from one to four. Give each group a rhythm instrument, such as a bongo drum, tambourine, or triangle. Have each group choose a song, and show them how to play the rhythm of their song (the first line is sufficient) on their instrument.

Before play begins, choose four points in the play space that are a good distance from each other and mark them with a stick or flag. Ask all of the "number ones" to go stand by the first marker, all of the "number twos" to stand by the second

marker, etc. Make sure that the child assigned to number one can play the rhythm of his song on his instrument.

When you make a signal, all of the "number ones" run as fast as they can to the second marker and play their rhythm for their "number two" teammate. Once the number two teammate has listened carefully enough so she can reproduce the rhythm, she takes the instrument and runs as fast as she can to the third marker and plays for the number three teammate. Teammate number three listens, takes the instrument, and runs to teammate four. Teammate four listens, takes the instrument and runs to you. Have each fourth teammate play the rhythm for you so you can check its accuracy.

The first group to reach you and correctly reproduce the rhythm is the winner.

Concentration Games

These games are closely related to listening games in the sense that listening plays an important part in them. However, they require a higher degree of attentiveness and discipline for successful play.

These games are often perceived as difficult or tiring because they require mental effort. For this reason, keep the play times short, and conduct them in a quiet, peaceful room where distractions are at a minimum.

Chief Characteristics of Concentration Games

- Group members must focus their attention on the action performed by you or another group member

- At the same time, you introduce disturbing or distracting sounds, which have to be blocked out by group members so they can hear what they need to hear

- The focus is usually on listening but may shift to seeing or feeling

- Often, a response is required of the participants, and they can only give the correct response if they are paying close attention

17

Feeling the Rhythm

Have the children sit in a circle. Ask one child to think of a song and, without saying anything, tap out the first line of the rhythm on her neighbor's back. Then the neighbor passes on to the child next to her the rhythm that she felt, and so on. Continue until the rhythm passes around the whole circle.

The last person to get the rhythm should clap it. Compare it to the original rhythm. Then have another child start a new rhythm.

Note: Usually the rhythm becomes different as it is passed around. Have the group discuss why. If the rhythm is too long or too difficult, ask for a simpler one on the next round. If the distortion is simply the result of poor attentiveness, ask the group to concentrate.

18

Clapping Game

Requires: One rhythm instrument

Divide the group in half. Have each half sit in a separate area. Pretend you are a metronome and beat out a regular and peaceful tempo on the rhythm instrument. When you signal, have both begin counting from the same note. Now ask one group to clap on the fifth count, and the other group on the third count. See if they can keep this up for one or two minutes. Repeat it a few times until no one makes a mistake.

Then ask one person to deliberately clap at the wrong time to try to confuse the others. This can also be repeated a few times, with different members creating the disturbance.

Next, try this game using three groups. Group A, for example, can clap on the fifth count, Group B on the fourth, and Group C on the third. Once group members no longer make a mistake, ask someone to create a disturbance. Little by little, you can also increase the tempo.

Note: This game is more difficult than it seems and at the beginning the tempo should be slow. Have the groups change their count regularly so that they do not simply clap by rote.

Variation 1: Once the game is going well, add instruments. Try giving one group drums, another xylophones, and another rattles and bells.

19

The Square of Sounds

Requires: Blackboard and chalk or markers and an easel

Draw a large square on the board and divide it into four rows of four. Ask each participant (but no more than 16) to think of a sound and write it in one of the squares. The sounds can be expressed as notes of the scale, written words, etc. Use a different sound for each square and try leaving a square or two empty.

Consider the finished result a musical score in four-four time. Ask group members to read from left to right and vocalize the sounds as you point to the squares. Make sure no sound is made when you point to the empty squares. When you reach the last square, return to the first and start again, and repeat the sequence several times.

As the group "gets" the sequence, gradually speed up the tempo, otherwise attention will wander. This whole exercise can only succeed if everyone strictly adheres to the rhythm.

Now try to do this without pointing at the squares but by clapping or tapping out the bars.

If this goes well, try performing the piece as a round. Divide the group into two subgroups. Have one half begin at the top line and the second half start at the top once the first group reaches the third line. This gives you a two-part round.

Variation 1: Introduce instruments, work on rhythm, or try rounds that have three or four parts. Do not worry about keeping it in four-four time only; you can also point to the squares in a completely free-tempo way.

20

Musical Hand-in-Hand

Requires: An instrument for each person

Seat group members in a circle. Give each person an instrument and have them make up their own short tune or rhythm using it. The short piece should lend itself to being continually repeated.

Ask everyone to play together, at first. Then, when you make a sign, half the members of the group should switch and play the tune of somebody else, such as the person sitting next to them. Now you have two people playing each song.

Make a sign again and have different pairs join in with other pairs, so that songs are being played by four people each. Then have the groups of four become groups of eight. Repeat this sequence until the whole group is playing the same song. Then find out who created the song that survived this process.

21

Dialing Rhythms

Requires: An instrument for each person, blackboard and chalk or markers and an easel, index cards numbered 1 through 5

Write up four or five simple rhythms on the board, like these below.

Number them. (If there are more than sixteen children in the group, you will need five rhythms.) Practice the rhythms with the whole group until every member can recognize each rhythm and play it.

Then give each child an index card with a number made up of two or three digits (such as 213 or 142). This refers to a combination of the numbered rhythms and is their "telephone number." The children can use these rhythm sequences to "telephone" each other.

Have one child begin by "dialing" any number, using his instrument to play the appropriate rhythm. The child who recognizes that number as hers responds by "dialing" another number, and so on.

The children need to play close attention at all times so they can hear if their numbers are "called"; they also need to reproduce the rhythms carefully for the game to work well.

22

Cacophony Without Laughing

Requires: Index cards with titles of songs written on them

Divide the players into groups of three. Each group takes a turn to play while the others look on.

Give each member of the first group an index card with the title of a different well-known song written on it. When you give the sign, have each group member sing the song on his or her index card. They must do this without laughing. Decide in advance whether they should sing the whole song or only one verse. Anyone who laughs gets a forfeit.

Then have the other groups take their turn, preferably with different songs. The group with the fewest forfeits wins.

23

Rhythm Game

Requires: An instrument for each person

Have group members select an instrument and make up a short rhythm. Then have someone play his rhythm. The person next to him repeats this rhythm and plays her own. The next person repeats *both* rhythms and adds a third. Continue in this way until everyone has a chance to add his or her own rhythm. See how far you get.

24

Mirror with Sound

Requires: A CD or cassette player or radio

Divide the group into pairs and have them face each other. Play some gentle music and ask one person from each pair to move in time to the music, then have her partner mirror her movements. The pair should stand in place while they do this.

Turn off the music and ask one person in each pair to make vocal sounds, musical or other, which the partner mimics. You can also combine movement and sound. Have them attune the sound to the movement as much as possible. After a few minutes ask the group to change partners.

25

Human Xylophone

Requires: Groups of eight

Have the eight people in each group stand in line and ask the first person to sing a low note and memorize it. The next person sings the next higher note on the major scale, the next the third, etc. In this way, each person in the line sings a note from the first note to the octave above. Have each person remember his own note so he can sing it at any time. Consider this line of eight people a human xylophone with eight keys.

Now have each person hold out one hand so that other group members can take turns tapping or pressing the different hands and playing the xylophone. Each person must continue singing his note for as long as his hand is pressed. Members of the group may play well-known songs, improvise, or even try two-part songs using more than one "xylophone."

26

Putting a Song Together

Requires: A specific number of people, depending on the complexity of the song used. For instance, a song with eight lines would need nine players.

Ask one person to go out of the room. Then split a well-known song into a number of sections. Allocate one section, or line, to each person. When everyone has her piece of the song, have the group move to different places in the room.

Ask the first person to return. When she does, have group members sing their own section over and over again. The person must try to establish what the song is, and place group members in a row so that the sections of the song are in the correct order. When the last person is in place, each member of the group then sings his line or section in turn and the first person checks to make sure that the order is correct.

Variation: Make this game more difficult by singing la-la-la or humming the tune instead of singing the words.

27

The Story of Sounds

Requires: A variety of musical instruments

Seat group members in a circle around a variety of musical instruments. Ask one member to begin by saying a sentence that ends with a sound. The sound is not spoken, but played on the instrument.

The person next to him repeats the sentence—and sound—and adds a new sentence with a new sound. The sentences should link together to form a story. For example, one person could start by saying, "I was walking through the town and I heard (sound of a horn)." The next person could add, "On a side street, I saw a peddler sitting in his cart and I heard (sound of a bell)." The third person would repeat all of this and add a new sentence and sound.

See how far you can get.

It is best to leave the instruments in the center so that they are available for the next person.

Musical Quizzes

Quizzes offer many possibilities. Thanks to TV game shows they have also become quite popular. Young people are motivated by the competitive element in these games, which provides them with an exciting opportunity to measure their skills against others.

In addition to encouraging memory and recall, quiz games help group members to practice the art of remaining focused. Quizzes can also be used to introduce a project or conclude an exercise and see what work still needs to be done. In such cases you should address the questions, tasks, or assignments to a specific subject or theme. You can also give quizzes to draw out the imagination and creativity of the participants.

However you choose to use a quiz, remember to offer the winner a reward, even if it is only a symbolic one. Otherwise you will lose much of the excitement of the game. Winners can be individuals or groups.

Keep in mind that a musical quiz can require considerable preparation. You may need to make tapes, create questions and assignments, establish a scoring system, choose a jury, etc. You can also get the group to set up the quiz for you, but make sure you give them plenty of time to do it.

Chief Characteristics

There are three main forms of musical quizzes. They are:

- **Listening Quizzes.** These require players to recognize snatches of music that you play live or from a cassette. Try using well-known songs or compositions, or tapes of recognizable urban sounds.

- **Activity Quizzes.** Let the group form smaller subgroups and assign each subgroup an activity. Give the groups a short time to prepare, then have them present their activity to a jury. Let them know that the emphasis in scoring will be on the imaginative quality of their expression.

- **Question Quizzes.** This is the simplest form of a quiz. Prepare a series of questions that can be answered individually or by members of the group.

You can also create games that combine all three forms of quizzes.

28

Listening Quiz

Requires: A tape recorder, a tape of short bits of music, pen, and paper for each group member. Each musical piece should last about one minute.

Play a piece to the group, then ask them a question about it. Allow them 30 seconds to think about their answers. Here are some suggested recordings and questions. Modify them to suit the music you have available, and the age and interests of the group.

Question: What is the name of this group?

Tape: A blues number
Question: What kind of music is this?

Tape: A recording of the Greek *sirtaki*
Question: What is the country of origin?

Tape: A song from a musical such as "Annie"
Question: Which musical does this song come from?

Tape: A song from a popular rock group
Question: What is the name of this group?

Tape: A recording of Spanish flamenco guitar
Question: What kind of dance is done to this music?

Tape: "Don't Come Around Here No More" by Tom Petty and the Heartbreakers
Question: Which Eastern instrument is being played in this song?

Tape: "The Flight of the Bumblebee" by Rimsky-Korsakov
Question: Which creature is being portrayed in this music?

29

Activity Quiz

Requires: An instrument for each person, and a large group that can be subdivided into groups of three or four

Divide the group into smaller groups of three or four. Ask the groups to perform musical activities, which may be undertaken by a whole subgroup or just one member from a group. Decide how many minutes of preparation time you will allow and state this clearly before each task. Also specify how many points can be earned for each task.

Here are examples of activities you can ask:

1. Who can clap the rhythm of a tango?

2. Who can impersonate a conductor?

3. Who can use an instrument to imitate an animal?

4. Who can sing the highest?

5. Who can imitate a Spanish dancer (while the others in the group clap the rhythm)?

6. Without laughing, sing three or four songs all at the same time.

7. How many different sounds around you can you name in 30 seconds?

8. Who can sing the first verse of the top song in the week's Top Ten?

9. Who can do an impersonation of a well-known singer?

10. Who can hold a note the longest?

30

Question Quiz

Requires: Pens and paper

The aim of this quiz is to give participants insight into the commercial aspects of pop music. Consequently, the discussion after the quiz is more important than the correct response to the questions. Because the music scene changes every year look up the information you need or consult a local music critic.

1. Name the song that sold the greatest number of records last year and the group that recorded it.

2. How many singles must be sold before a record goes gold?

3. For how many weeks, on average, does a single stay in the Top Ten? What is the longest you know?

4. Why do we have record charts or lists of hits?

5. How much does a record store earn on the sale of an average-priced cassette or CD?

6. How much money does a group or recording artist get for every album sold?

7. What is a "white" recording?

8. How much can a professional pop music group earn per performance? What is the range?

9. How much does a disc jockey earn in an evening?

10. Name three solo singers of commercial music.

31

Countries Quiz

Requires: A tape recorder with taped bits of music, pens, and paper

Prepare about 10 recordings of well-known international songs in advance. Alternatively, you could sing them

Examples:

Havah Naguilah (Israel)
Cielito Lindo (Mexico)
O, Susannah (United States)
O Tannenbaum (Germany)
Frere Jacques (France)
Hare Krishna (India)
Perompompom (Spain)
Santa Lucia (Italy)
Greensleeves (England)
Nkosi Sikelel'i Afrika (South Africa)

Have each group member write the name of the song and the country of its origin. See who can most quickly identify the correct name and country for each song by calling it out as the song is played.

Variation 1: To make this game a little more difficult, don't include lyrics with the melodies. Play instrumental recordings or sing them using la-la-la instead of words.

Variation 2: For a younger age group use different, simpler songs and just have them name the countries, or sing the first line and have them complete the tune.

Games that Develop Social Skills

Games for Introductions and Getting to Know Each Other

These games are excellent for creating a friendly and relaxed atmosphere and providing an informal, easy way for people to get to know each other. They also encourage spontaneity and are fun.

Use them when a group is new and members do not yet feel at ease with each other. You can also use these games to bring in the element of movement, which can add a new dimension of engagement.

Chief Characteristics

- These games are true group games because the group plays together.

- Nobody can feel a failure in these games, because everyone plays as part of a group.

- Most of these games have a simple framework and are of short duration.

- The games are often based on well-known games such as musical chairs, tag, and "go fish."

32

Jamming Station

Requires: At least six players, a few instruments, a whistle, a room where you can make noise without disturbing others

Divide the group into three equal teams. The first team is the transmitter, the second is the receiver, the third is the jamming station. Have the transmitting team move to one wall of the room and the receiving team move to the opposite wall. Place the jamming team and the musical instruments between the other two teams.

The transmitters start the game by choosing a well-known song and "transmitting" it by singing only the notes. No words are to be used. The receivers have to try to recognize the song as quickly as possible. The jammers in the middle try to "jam" or confuse the receivers by making as much noise as possible with the instruments.

Use a loud whistle to signal the start of each turn. Set a limit, say 30 to 60 seconds, by which time the receivers must recognize the song. After the time limit blow the whistle again. If the receivers guess the song correctly, record how much time they take. If they are unable to guess, record the maximum time. Rotate the group roles so that each team has three turns being the receiver and see which team takes the shortest time to guess the songs being transmitted.

Note: People can really let themselves go in this game—which makes it so enjoyable. Take into account the fact that neighbors will react to the noise!

33

Instruments Dance

Requires: An instrument for each person except one, a CD or cassette player

Stand the group in a circle and place instruments around the outside of the circle. When you turn on the music, everyone walks or dances around the circle. When you stop the music, everyone grabs an instrument. The person who doesn't get one waits for the others to return theirs, then selects one. When play starts again she steps out of the circle and plays her instrument to accompany the recorded music.

The next person who doesn't get an instrument also plays to accompany the music, and so on. This continues until everyone in the group—but one—has an instrument and is accompanying the record. The person who stayed in the longest wins the round and could be given a special role in the next game, such as controlling the recorded music or suggesting variations.

Note: Gradually, group members form an "orchestra." This game is actually a good way to get people to improvise without making them self-conscious about the fact that they are improvising, or that they have never done improvisation together. You could develop the orchestra further by letting them improvise independently of the recorded music or by singing along with them, or by having the orchestra try Game 60 (on page 87).

34

Look for Your Own Song

Requires: A group of at least six to nine, index cards with song titles written on them, a whistle

Prepare enough index cards for each member of the group. Then choose three well-known songs and write on each index card the title of one of the songs. Make sure that there are the same number of cards for each song. Then fold the cards, put them in an open container, shake it, and have the group members pick one each.

When you blow the whistle, have each person walk around the room singing the song on his index card. As they walk, group members listen for others who are singing their song. Once they find them, they link hands and keep walking and singing. This continues until three groups are formed.

Note: This game cannot stand alone. Once you have formed the groups you have to do something with them. You could continue by putting one group in the middle of the room and letting them sing their own song while the second group accompanies them with instruments and the third group improvises a dance. Then get them to change roles twice.

35

Instrument Tag

Requires: A different instrument for each person, a rolled-up newspaper, chairs, a blackboard and chalk or markers and an easel

Have each player choose a musical instrument. Repeat the names of the players and their instruments a few times so that everyone is clear on who has chosen what instrument. Then have the players sit in a circle with their instruments in front of them and their hands on their knees.

The game starts with one person standing in the middle of the circle with a rolled-up newspaper. A person who is sitting calls out the name of another person and his instrument. The person with the newspaper has to try as quickly as possible to tap the hands of that person, who must try to name another person and her instrument before being tapped. If he succeeds, he stays where he is. If he is tagged first, he has to change places with the person in the middle.

Note: If the group is younger and needs a memory aid, put the names of the players and instruments on the blackboard. The tension in this game creates enthusiastic players, at least at first. Draw the game to a close as soon as the attention slackens.

Variation 1: If the group is quite large and you have a bigger circle, the person whose name is called has to pick up his instrument and play at least one note before he is tagged.

36

Songs of Animal Sounds

Requires: A group of at least nine players

Seat the group in a circle. Choose a simple, well-known song or nursery rhyme and sing it through once. Divide the players into smaller groups of two or three and let each group think of an animal sound that can be used to sing the song. Have them try it out to see if it works, and make sure each group has chosen a different sound.

Then take the role of conductor and point to each group, asking them to sing just one line in their chosen animal sound. The aim is for them to sing it in the right time and rhythm.

If Group A has chosen "moo," Group B, "woof," and Group C, "meow," try pointing to Group B for line 1, Group A for line 2, Group C for line 3, then Group A for line 4, etc.

Note: This game nearly always produces a comical effect. Consider it a good warm-up and don't spend too long on it. If it goes on for too long, it stops being fun.

37

My Instrument

Requires: Chairs, blackboard and chalk or markers and an easel

Seat the group in a circle and have everyone choose the name of a different instrument. Repeat the names of the players and their instruments a few times so that everyone is clear who has chosen what instrument. Then have the group repeat a sequence of four movements: clapping the left hand on the left knee, clapping the right hand on the right knee, pointing the left thumb over the left shoulder, and pointing the right thumb over the right shoulder. The movements should be done at a slow but regular pace and in four-four time. Practice before you begin in earnest.

Here is the next sequence: Have one person in the group name her instrument at the precise moment that everyone is pointing over their left shoulder. Then, when everyone is pointing over their right shoulder, she names the instrument of someone else. Nothing at all should be said when group members are clapping, which is the first movement in this four-movement sequence.

The person whose instrument has been named goes next.

If anyone makes a mistake or misses the rhythm, take her out of the game and "retire" her instrument.

Note: If the group is younger and needs a memory aid, put the names of the players and instruments on the blackboard. This is a good game for developing rhythm skills, but it can become frustrating if it goes on too long.

38

Musical Hats

Requires: Hat, chairs, CD or cassette player

Place the chairs in a closed circle, one behind the other. Have the players circle around the chairs. Put a hat on the head of one person. When the music starts, the person with the hat puts it on the head of the person in front of her, who then passes it along in the same way. When the music stops, the person wearing the hat is out and must leave the circle and take a chair with her. The hat is given to her neighbor and play continues, until only one person is left.

Note: This is a variation of musical chairs. It is ideal for parties and social events. The last person can receive a prize or play a special role in the next activity.

39

Musical Tag

Requires: Two instruments of each kind, an outside area suitable for playing "hide-and-go-seek"

Divide players into two equal groups and give each group the same set of instruments. Tell Group A to take their instruments and hide outside. When they have hidden, Group B comes out, and each member of the group sends out a signal with his or her instrument. The signal should be answered by the person in Group A who has the same instrument. Members of Group B then use the sound to try to track down and tag the person in Group A who has the same instrument. Those who are "caught" stand in an open area. When a round is complete and everyone in Group A is tagged, the groups switch roles.

Note: You need good weather to play this game. Organize it in a wooded area where other people will not be disturbed.

40

"I Am Sitting in the Grass and I Hear..."

Requires: A chair for each person and an extra chair

Seat the group on a circle of chairs, leaving one chair empty. Have everyone choose the name of an instrument and announce it to the group.

The game works like this: The person who is sitting next to the empty chair begins. She gets up and, as she moves to the empty chair, says, "I am sitting...." The person next to her says "in the grass..." as he quickly moves to her empty chair. The next person in the circle continues "and I hear..." as she moves into *his* empty chair. The fourth person, as he moves to the empty chair, makes the sound of one of the instruments. The person who chose that instrument now goes and sits on the empty chair.

When this happens, the whole sequence is repeated. The person now sitting next to the newly vacated chair begins again with "I am sitting...," and so on. This is repeated until someone misses his or her line, responds to someone else's instrument name, or, in the opinion of the leader, reacts too slowly. When this happens, that person leaves the circle and takes a chair with him. Play until there are three or four people left, or time runs out. Make sure people get a chance to play as a group for a while before beginning to eliminate players.

Note: Give clear instructions before starting about which direction players should move. Otherwise, misunderstandings can easily arise. Also, ask everybody to make the sound of his or her chosen instrument in advance.

41

Changing Instruments

Requires: Percussion instruments and sticks (one less than the number of players), index cards with song titles written on them, a whistle, space outside or a large room

Scatter the instruments over the area, not too closely together. Attach to each instrument a card with the title of a well-known song, and place a stick next to each instrument. Choose one person to be "It" and have the others stand next to an instrument.

When you blow the whistle, have each member play the rhythm of the song written on the card, using the stick. When they finish they put the stick down and, when another player finishes, they try to exchange instruments with him or her. Then they play the song that goes with the new instrument, before exchanging instruments again.

The person who is It tries to grab one of the sticks that has been put down before a player who is exchanging instruments can pick up the stick again. Whoever gets the stick first has a right to the instrument, and the other person becomes It.

Note: The groups will end up playing the songs faster and faster. Don't object.

42

Key Dance

Requires: A large table, instruments, a key

Have the players sit in a circle with their hands under the table. Start a song everyone knows. While everyone is singing, pass a key around under the table. The person who has the key in her hands on the last word of the song is out. She must leave the table, take a musical instrument, and accompany the singers. Use a new song each time. The person who stays in the longest wins.

43

Singing Tag

Requires: Space outside

Stake out a play area of approximately 15 by 30 yards. Use a boundary line to divide the space in half, so that you have two equal square areas.

Divide the players into two equal groups and give each group their own area. Have a player from Group 1 take a deep breath and keep singing a note that is clearly audible. He may not interrupt the note to take a breath, or for any other reason.

While singing the note, he runs into the other group's territory and tries to tag as many people there as he can. Those who are tagged are out and have to leave their area. The singer has to get back to his own side before his note runs out. If he doesn't make it back to his own side before his breath runs out, then *he* is out and the people he tagged get to rejoin their group.

Players in the team being tagged may dodge, duck, and run away from the singer as long as they stay within their own area. Anyone who steps out of the area in any direction—including the singer—is automatically out.

After this a singer from Group 2 goes into Group 1's area to tag them. This continues until all the players on one team have been tagged, and the other team wins.

Variation 1: If the singer runs out of breath and stops singing before he gets back to his own side and someone from the other team tags him, then the singer is out and everyone he tagged is free and can rejoin the game.

44

Instrument "Go Fish"

Requires: 16 to 20 blank cards about the size of playing cards or a little bigger

Make four or five sets of four cards. On each set draw an instrument, so that you have, for example, four cards with a bongo drum, four with a guitar, four with a kazoo, etc. For each set use four different colors, so that you have a red, yellow, green, and blue bongo, etc.

Shuffle the cards and deal them out to the group. The aim is to make up complete sets. When one player asks another for a card, she should specify the color and make the sound of the instrument requested. Establish these sounds in advance. A drum could be "boom boom," a bongo, "tacka, tacka, tacka," a triangle, "ting, ting."

If the player asking makes the sound correctly and the person being asked has the card, the asker receives the card and can take another turn. If she makes a mistake in the sound or is asking for a card the other player doesn't have, the player being asked gets a turn. The winner is the person who collects the most sets of four.

45

Rhythms "Go Fish"

Requires: Four or five instruments, 16 or 20 cards about the size of playing cards or a little bigger

Make four or five sets of four cards. On each set draw an instrument that you have available for the game. Beside each instrument, write out one of four rhythms, such as:

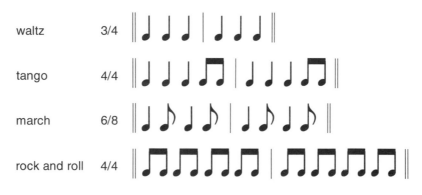

For each instrument in the set choose a *different* rhythm, so that each card shows a different combination of instrument and rhythm.

Place the instruments in the middle of the circle of players. Shuffle the cards and deal them. Each player tries to collect as many sets of four as he can. This is done by asking another player for a card, and playing on the instrument they want from her in a particular rhythm. If, for example, someone wants the tango rhythm on the bongo, he must pick up the bongos and play the tango rhythm. The different rhythms must be clearly defined in advance and practiced if necessary. The game continues in the same way as Game 44.

46

Living "Go Fish"

Requires: Index cards and pens, blackboard and chalk or markers and an easel

Give each player an index card on which they write the name of a well-known singer. Have them fold the index cards and return them to you without telling anyone the name they have chosen. During the game, each person becomes that singer.

Next, divide the group into four or five smaller groups and seat them away from each other. Read out the singers' names aloud or write them on a blackboard. If any name appears twice, both people have to hand in a new name.

Designate one group to begin. Members of that group ask for a singer from any other group. If the singer is in that group, she must move to the first group. If the singer is not there then the second group gets to ask for a singer. The game is over when one group brings everyone together.

Note: This game can provide animated discussion of the rules. For example, should the person who changes groups be in solidarity with the new group or the old group? If the question arises during play, make an ad hoc decision so play can continue.

Variation 1: If the first group "turns up" the singer in the other group, they have to sing a song associated with or recorded by that singer to get her to join their group.

Interaction Games

The point of these games is to teach the members of the group to respond to each other in a more structured way, even though the results are not prescribed. Be less concerned with the results here than with the quality of group interaction. These games challenge players to respond to the initiative of others, take initiative themselves, and pay attention to each other.

Because movement and dancing is involved, interactive games hold particular attraction for young children.

Chief Characteristics

- These are movement games with a fairly free structure.

- Music is not essential but does offer support. It helps to get the game going.

- These games are exclusively concerned with interaction. They have almost nothing to do with an end product or a winner.

47

Living Mirror

Requires: An even number of players, a CD or cassette player

Have players stand in pairs, facing each other. Place the pairs far enough apart so that one pair does not disturb another.

Have the pairs decide who will lead first. When the music starts, the leader makes slow and gentle movements with his arms and upper body, and the follower mirrors the movements as closely as possible, in the same direction and at the same time.

Both should stay in place. Make sure the movements are slow and gliding. After a few minutes, have the other partner lead.

Note: Players may be inclined to go too fast. If so, slow them down. You could use those who do this particularly well as models for the rest of the group.

48

Making a Shape

Requires: CD or cassette player

Play gentle music. Have the group walk freely around the room in time to the music. When the music stops name a shape, such as a circle. Have the group form it as quickly as possible. Take note of how long they need to make an acceptably round circle without discussing anything in advance. If it takes too long, have them try again to see if they can do it more quickly. Do the same with other shapes, such as a straight line, a square, a half-moon, or a triangle.

Note: This game is particularly good for helping you recognize the status of different children in the group. Who suggests how things should be done, and who supports them? Observations like this can be discussed afterward, if appropriate.

49

Statue!

Requires: CD or cassette player

Give a number to each member of the group and let players walk around in a circle in time to music. At a sign from you, Player 1 goes into the middle of the circle and takes a particular pose. She can stand, sit, or recline. Have her freeze in this pose for the rest of the game.

When she is ready she gives a signal and Player 2 strikes her own pose, touching or making contact with Player 1. Player 2 signals to Player 3, and so on. Make sure everyone who goes into the center makes contact with at least one of those who is already there. Keep going until all the players have created a complex statue.

Note: Children are always delighted to have their picture taken at the final moment. Have a camera ready to produce a group shot!

50

Leading and Following

Requires: An even number of players, a CD or cassette player

The players stand in pairs anywhere in the room, and each pair designates a leader and a follower. The leader holds up his right hand about shoulder high with his palm outward, and his partner puts the palm of his left hand against it without holding, just touching. With the leaders leading, all the pairs move around the room together in time to the music. The movement can be high or low, walking or turning, etc., and they must both make sure that the hand contact is not broken. Every few minutes they should change leaders without stopping.

Variation: Have the pairs try this game without touching. Ask them to pretend that two ropes connect their hands, and to make sure that during movement their hands stay the same distance apart.

51

Which Way Shall I Go?

Requires: A group of three or multiples of three, a blindfold

Have two people stand about eight to ten yards apart. Blindfold the third person and place her exactly halfway between them. The person wearing the blindfold should not know where the other two are. The other two try to attract her by means of sound. Every time the blindfolded person hears a sound that attracts her she moves a step closer to it; but if she dislikes it, she moves a step away. If the sound has no effect, she stays still. Both players try to get her to come to them as quickly as possible. When the person with the blindfold reaches one person, the three switch roles.

Note: In the discussion afterward, explore the idea of attraction and repulsion or dislike for certain sounds. Ask the person who wore the blindfold if she knew who was making the sounds and if this influenced her choices.

52

Persuasion Game

Have each player choose a well-known song and keep it to himself. At a sign from you, everyone walks crisscross around the room singing his song as loud as possible. Each person should try to persuade the others to switch over to his song, by singing louder, choosing a more attractive song, etc. Allow two minutes for play. When you stop, see who has managed to get the biggest group together.

Note: Do this in a place where you will not disturb others. This game is noisy!

53

Instruments Lead

Requires: Different instruments for half the players in the group

Divide the players into two groups and give an instrument to each of the players in one group. Have the players in the other group stand anywhere in the room.

Seat the group with the instruments in a row or half-circle so that they are clearly visible to the others. Then assign each person in the second group an instrument to follow. This person will be directed by that instrument; for instance, one beat means to make a step, a fast tempo means to move quickly. The idea is to get people to attune themselves to the instrument and follow it as closely as possible.

After a while have the groups switch, so each person in the second group gets to play the instrument she was following.

Note: Some players may want to play as quickly as possible, but point out that when it is their turn their partner could easily take revenge!

54

Completing Songs

Seat the group in a circle. Have someone sing the first line of a song, the next person sing the next line, and so on. Continue until someone does not know the next line. This person introduces another song until, again, someone doesn't know the next line. Continue for as long as the group finds this enjoyable.

55

Reacting Game

Requires: An instrument for each person

All the players sit in a circle after taking an instrument. One by one, have them play something on their instrument. Ask the first person to play something quite short. The idea is for everyone to play for exactly the same length of time as the person before them. At some point, ask the player to increase the length of the piece. Later, increase it still more. Alternately, the playing can be completely free, with anyone playing for any length.

Note: This game lends itself to being repeated because each time it produces something different. Another good idea is to have the players exchange instruments regularly. Stop the game when the players' attention begins to wander.

56

Dialogue with Sounds

Requires: A quiet room

Ask the players to walk slowly around the room, thinking of a sound they like. At a signal from you, have them make their sound aloud, repeating it constantly and yet remaining aware of the sounds the others are making. Ask everyone to look for a partner whose sound complements his own. Together they have to make a dialogue of sounds. When everyone has found a partner, they all sit in a large circle, while continuing their separate dialogues.

You can now point to different partners in random order to increase their volume while others go softer. In this way you can create a piece of music that assimilates all of the dialogues, and can even be taped. Ask other players to do this also, and observe the different sequences they try.

Note: This game requires concentration and creativity. It can also be done with instruments, with each person finding a sound he or she likes on an instrument and choosing partners in this way. It may be better in some cases to begin with this variation.

57

Producing a Story

Requires: A tape or cassette recorder and a microphone

Seat the group in a circle around the microphone. Have each person say a sentence into the microphone so that each sentence follows the one before and creates a story. When everyone has had a turn, play the recording back to the group. Did it work? What do you need to do to complete the story line?

Variation: Have the group come up with an ending and record the best version, or write individual endings for the story.

58

Rhymin' Simon

Requires: An even number of players

Seat the group in two rows facing each other. Have one person make up a sentence that the person opposite must match with a rhyme. For instance, Player 1 says, "Last week, I walked into town." Player 2 follows, "But I slipped on the road and fell down." Then continue down the row, and back again. The first time around, the sentences can be chosen at random. The next time, however, the players should try to continue the first pair's rhymes or meaning and create complete verses.

59

Musical Puppets

Requires: A group of at least seven or eight, and four clearly different instruments such as bongos, tambourine, xylophone, and cymbals

Hand out the instruments to about half the group and have the other half act as puppets. In a large room there can be more puppets. Agree, in advance, on four clear signals to which the puppets must react. The sound of each instrument represents a certain movement for the puppets, for example:

bongos: walk forward till the next signal
tambourine: walk backward till the next signal
xylophone: move arms up and down
cymbals: turn around

Depending on the group, you could make the signals as simple or complex as they like.

The four people playing the instruments must remain aware of each other, so they do not give different or opposing signals at the same time. After a while, have the musicians and puppets change places.

Note: If a group likes this game, they can play it regularly and develop more signals that they all share and understand.

Trust Games

These are important games that are fundamentally different from previous games in this book. They contribute to the development of trust, as much within the individual as between those in the group. They also strengthen each person's confidence about being accepted by the group and receiving group support when necessary.

These games are not well-suited for groups that have just come together. Save them for when players know each other and are relaxed around each other.

One of the consequences of using these games is that group members gradually develop a sense of safety with each other. They feel, *I can be myself here and be accepted as I am.* With this feeling, the creative process in the group is enhanced and each person's ideas are welcomed, and more freely expressed.

Chief Characteristics

- Trust games are often nonverbal, meaning there is no need to speak during the games. Keeping them nonverbal removes many barriers such as pretense and rationalization, differences of opinion and interpretation, and hostile criticism.

- Body contact often plays an important part.

- Much of the work is done in pairs. This decreases fear and offers the possibility of mutual contact.

- As a rule, the group—or part of the group—takes responsibility for one individual (usually the one who is wearing the blindfold), who may need support. This stimulates the development of mutual responsibility within the group.

60

Hot and Cold

Requires: A blindfold, enough instruments for all but one person

Blindfold one person and give instruments to the others. Ask the blindfolded person to find another person in the group, guided by the musicians. The person who is being "looked for" should pick a spot in the room and stay there. The others play louder when the blindfolded person is getting closer and softer when she is moving away from the target.

Before you start, rehearse what is meant by loud and soft. Also, make sure that the blindfolded player does not bump into anything. If this appears likely, turn her in another direction. Once the seeker finds the target, the target gets the blindfold.

Note: After the game ask players what it felt like to have the blindfold on.

Variation: Have two people as seekers and designate two others to be sought.

61

Obstacle Walk

Requires: An instrument for each person, a large room, a blindfold

Give each person in the group—except one—an instrument and have them stand scattered around the room like obstacles. They should stay in one spot, and not be too close to anyone else.

Blindfold the person without an instrument and ask her to walk through the room without touching anything. If she gets close to someone, he should make a warning noise on his instrument.

The blindfolded person should keep moving all the time. Make sure she doesn't bump into anything. Change players every few minutes.

Note: In this game it is not essential for everyone to have a turn. Stop after a few rounds of play because this game requires a lot of concentration and can get tiring.

62

Labyrinth

Requires: An instrument for each person, a blindfold, objects that can serve as obstacles, a large room

Have the group members form as large a circle as possible, standing at equal distances from each other. Each one has an instrument and makes up a short tune (or, if there aren't enough instruments, a player can make up and sing or hum a tune).

Blindfold one player and place him in the middle. His goal is to reach someone in the circle by following the sounds made by the group. He is led exclusively by the sounds made by the group—that is to say, he should take just one step in the direction of each sound he hears at any one moment, and the rest of the group should make just one sound at a time.

Group members need to remain alert so that only one person plays at a time, and the sounds do not follow each other too fast. When the player reaches someone in the circle, the two trade places.

Now put obstacles—chairs, bags, etc.—between the group and the person at the center of the circle. The people now have to organize their sounds in such a way that the blindfolded player does not bump into any obstacles. Step by step he is led by the sounds through the obstacles until he reaches someone in the circle. He then changes with that person. If, however, he bumps into something, he changes places with the person who gave the "dangerous" signal.

Variation: Many variations of this game are possible. You can work with long and short sounds: as long as the sound continues the person can keep walking; when it stops he must stand still until he hears another sound. Since this game requires much concentration, keep the overall play time fairly short.

63

What Is the Sound I Hear?

Requires: An even number of players, a large room, blindfolds for half the group

Divide the group into pairs. One member of each pair puts on a blindfold and the other gently leads her by the hand around the room. As they walk around, the one leading should make sounds using whatever objects are available. He can run his hand along the radiator, tap a glass, rustle a curtain, and so on. The blindfolded person has to guess from the sound where she is in the room. Only when she guesses correctly can they move on. After a few minutes, they can switch places.

Note: This game can be played throughout a whole building if you are set up for it.

64

The Pied Piper

Requires: An even number of players, a large room or outside space, blindfolds for half the group, instruments for the other half

As in the previous game, players form pairs. One person is blindfolded and the other leads, playing one note continuously on his instrument. The blindfolded one follows the sound, and so is led around the room without holding anyone's hand. The leader must take care that his "charge" does not bump into anything. After a couple of minutes, they switch roles.

65

Guided by Instruments

Requires: A group of at least six players, several blindfolds, four instruments

Blindfold one person and have four musicians lead her toward another person who is somewhere in the room. Agree in advance on a code. For instance, the sound of the triangle means *turn to the left*, the tambourine means *turn to the right*, the bongos mean *go forward*, and the bells mean *go backward*.

   The musicians need to consider the directions from the point of view of the blindfolded player, and may only make one sound at a time.

Note: Only six people can play at a time, but others can watch. Make sure that people regularly change roles.

Variation: When the target person is found, she can be blindfolded, join hands with the first blindfolded player, and move hand-in-hand to find a third player, and so on.

66

Being Received

Requires: CD or cassette player, a blindfold

Divide the group into two. Have one half stand with their backs to one wall of the room and the other half stand with their backs against the opposite wall. There should be nothing between them.

Blindfold one person and have him dance, in time to gentle music, from one wall to the other. Once he makes it to the other wall the people in that line should receive him warmly. He can then pass the blindfold to another person, who does the same thing in the opposite direction.

If this goes well, speed up the tempo of the music.

67

The Dancing Dervish

Requires: A CD or cassette player, a few jackets or blankets

Make a bed of jackets and blankets in one corner of the room. Have the group stand in a tight circle, shoulder to shoulder, around one person who keeps her eyes closed. Direct the person in the middle to start turning around and around in time to a slow waltz. The group should be careful to protect her from falling down. As soon as she seems to falter or lose her balance, three or four players should catch her, lift her up as high in the air as possible, and then place her upon the "bed" of jackets.

No one should speak during the game.

Note: This game is only appropriate for groups whose members have known each other for some time and have built trust. It takes courage to get past feeling dizzy and trust that the other players will keep you from getting hurt. Allow plenty of time to discuss the experience afterwards.

68

Dancing Blind

Requirements: An even number of group members, blindfolds

Divide the group into pairs; one person in the pair leads, the other, who is blindfolded, follows. The leader holds on to his partner's hands and leads him dancing around the room in time to gentle music. After a minute, they change roles.

Variation: The pairs sit on the ground facing each other and place the palms of their hands together. The one who leads begins to move his hands gently in the air while the other tries to follow as well as he can without losing contact.

69

Obstacle Course

Requires: Tables, chairs, six instruments, a stopwatch, a blind-fold

Before starting, set up an obstacle course using chairs, tables, cushions, etc. Create a code for the six instruments so they can be used to lead a player through the course, and practice it with the group. (See Game 65 for details on how to create a code.) Each person is blindfolded in turn and guided through the course by the musicians.

Note: Players might try to complete the course in the shortest time, or find creative ways to get through the obstacles. Those group members who are watching can participate by becoming part of the course or making sure that the blindfolded player does not trip or hurt herself.

70

Who's That?

Requires: Chairs, a blindfold

Have the group sit in a circle, and blindfold one person. Guide the blindfolded person so that she is standing behind someone, and have that person make noises. The person wearing the blindfold must guess, by the sounds, who she is standing behind. The person making the noises must continue to make sounds but can try to disguise who she is. If the blindfolded player guesses correctly, they trade places. If she is wrong, she is moved behind someone else and tries again.

Note: You can also play this game on the ground. The blindfolded person can sit next to the other players or directly in front of them.

71

Come Closer

Requires: An even number of players

Ask two people to stand opposite each other, about 10 to 15 feet apart. They both close their eyes and take turns making sounds. As one makes a sound the other moves forward according to the length of the sound. When one of them feels that they have gotten close enough, he says "Stop."

Watch to see how close people get to one another.

Variation: Use musical instruments to make the sounds.

72

Human Musical Instruments

Requires: A CD or cassette player, small groups of seven to nine people, a comfortable room

Play gentle, relaxing music on the CD or cassette. One person in the group lies on the ground. The others sit around her and place their hands lightly on her forehead or shoulders, arms, hands, and feet. They should make sure that she feels comfortable and safe. The person lying down should close her eyes and try to relax.

Gently, in time to the music, the seated players should begin to tap with their fingertips on their friend's body. No one should speak, unless the person lying down wants something changed or wants to stop.

After one or two minutes lift up the lying person, carry her slowly around the room, and place her down gently in a comfortable spot. Then give someone else a turn.

Games that Develop Creative Skills

Games for Self-Expression and Improvisation

Introduce these games when group members know each other and feel reasonably safe with each other. If you do not wait until everyone is comfortable, these games will pose too great a threat to those individuals who feel insecure. In fact, it could make them close up even more.

Introduced at the right moment, however, these games can advance the group considerably. They can help individual members over certain thresholds and strengthen their identity.

These games also help participants develop their ability to take risks, and give them a structure in which it is easier to express their own ideas and visions. Little by little, participants can develop confidence in their power of imagination and lose their fear of being judged. These games also help develop spontaneous and creative solutions to new and unforeseen situations.

Chief Characteristics

- These games call upon intuition, fantasy, inventiveness, daring, and spontaneity.

- Individuals introduce themselves to the group. Alternately, individual presentations can be made in groups of two or three.

- These games can last a long time, so you may need to keep a close watch on the time.

- In some situations, the demands of the game can pose too great a threat to a particular individual. Be alert to this and do what you can to help that person over the threshold. If it seems appropriate to adapt the rules, then do so.

73

Game for Feelings

Requires: Three instruments, index cards with feelings written on them, blackboard and chalk or markers and an easel

Write on the board seven or eight basic feelings, such as love, loneliness, happiness, sadness, etc. Also have available three different instruments capable of sufficient expression so that participants can use them to express these feelings.

Prepare three times as many cards as there are participants. Write each feeling you put on the board on three cards, then mark each of those three cards with a different instrument so that no two cards are the same. Finally, make a few duplicates for reserves and make a few "jokers" or wild cards.

When the cards are ready, shuffle them and deal them out, keeping a few in hand. Give everyone the same number of cards and ask them to keep their cards hidden. Then choose someone to begin.

That person selects a card and puts it face down. She then uses the instrument specified on the card to express the feeling

as accurately as possible. If the card reads "SADNESS —
PIANO," for example, the person expresses sadness using the
piano. The group tries to guess the feeling. If they guess
correctly, the player throws in her card. If they guess wrong,
the player draws an extra card. Whoever receives the joker is
free to choose what she wants to do. The players should try to
get rid of all their cards.

Note: This game is an excellent way for players to become
acquainted with the expressive potential of different instruments. However, it is not suitable for young children since
players need patience with each other. A group of 10 people
may need 30 minutes or more of play. You can simplify the
game by using a few basic feelings. Later, you can add more
feelings and make the game more complicated.

74

Brimming Over with Song

Requires: A large room

Divide the group in two. Have half the players stand with their backs to one wall and the others stand with their backs against the opposite wall. Have two players from each side start singing as they walk from one wall to the other. Their singing should be freely improvised. When a player reaches the opposite wall, he tags someone, who is to begin her own improvisation with the last note of the person who tagged her.

Players can also combine suggested movements with their songs.

75

Acting Out a Proverb

Requires: Instruments if available, index cards with proverbs written on them

Divide the players into smaller groups of three or four. In turn, give each group a card with a well-known proverb (such as, "the squeaky wheel gets the grease"). The group gets 5 to 10 minutes to prepare, then they must "act out" their proverb by making a series of sounds on their instruments (or with their voices). The other groups try to guess the proverb.

Note: The groups could choose their own proverb. It should, however, contain some reference to sound.

76

Fantasy Instruments

Requires: A large paper bag

Have group members sit in a circle and pass around the paper bag. Ask each person to take an imaginary instrument out of the bag. When everyone has their imaginary instrument, go around the circle and have individuals demonstrate their instrument, using movement and sound. The others must try to guess the instrument.

Variation: All the fantasy instruments could play a tune together.

77

Musical Amplification

Seat the players in a circle and ask everyone to think of a sound. Have one person begin by softly making his sound. The person next to him repeats that sound a little louder, and the next person does the same even louder, and so on. Continue until you have gone around the circle. Have the next person start a new round with a new soft sound.

Note: Make sure the amplification is gradual, otherwise there won't be room to increase the volume after three or four players. Encourage participants to push their voices as far as they can.

78

Musical Forfeits

Requires: Index cards with musical assignments written on them, a large sheet or bag

Select players from the group by drawing lots or by using the results of another game. Have them forfeit something—like their shoe, belt, or purse—to you. Place these objects under a cover or in a large bag and then take them out one at a time from the cover. To win the object back the owner must pick a card and fulfill the musical assignment written on it to the satisfaction of the rest of the group.

Possible assignments include: dance a waltz with a partner; imitate a punk rock singer; sing the first song you ever learned.

79

Acting Out a Song

Requires: Index cards with song titles written on them, at least nine players

Form groups of three or four and give each group a card with the name of a well-known song on it. Tell the groups that they have to act out the first verse of the song, and give them 10 minutes to prepare. They cannot use words but they can do it in the form of a charade or tableau vivant. Have the groups take turns giving their short presentations while the others try to guess the song.

80

Sound and Feeling

Requires: As many instruments as possible, blackboard and chalk or markers and an easel, dice

Write two series of six words on the board. The first series should describe different ways to make sounds. For example: (1) high, (2) low, (3) sharp, (4) soft, (5) loud, and (6) flat. The second series should refer to basic feelings, such as: (1) cheerfulness, (2) fear, (3) depression, (4) anger, (5) tenderness, and (6) power.

The group sits in a circle and each person throws the dice in turn. The thrower chooses one number for the first series of words, and the second number for the second set of words, and expresses the combination musically on an instrument of his choice. If someone rolls a two and a five for instance, he can express low notes in a tender way or express fear loudly. If the rest of the group approves, his turn is complete. If not, he has to throw the dice again.

81

Singsong Gobbledy-Gook

Requires: Index cards with assignments written on them

Seat the group in a circle. Each person gets an index card with a different situation written on it, such as: "your bicycle has a flat tire" or "your ear aches." Each person takes a turn to stand in the middle of the circle and express their situation to the group using gestures and singsong gobbledy-gook—gibberish and nonsense words, half-spoken, half-sung. When someone in the group guesses correctly, the next person goes.

82

Music Charades

Divide the players into smaller groups of three or four and give each group a number. Ask Group 1 to think up a song for Group 2, Group 2 think up a song for Group 3, and so on, but tell the groups not to share the names of the songs. Instead, have Group 1 put Group 2 into positions which express a scene or line from the song. Then have Group 3 guess as quickly as possible what the song is. When they know, the members of Group 2 have to sing the song. Then have Group 2 do the same with Group 3, and so on.

83

The Sound Machine

Requires: Many different instruments, blackboard and chalk or markers and an easel, sheets of paper, pens

Draw an imaginary machine on the board. It should be a freewheeling combination of gears, cylinders, pumps, wheels with belts, etc. Whatever it is, it should suggest something capable of making a lot of movement and noise.

Divide the players into groups of four or five. Give each group a sheet of paper and a number of instruments. Have each group use their instruments to produce the most dominant sounds they think the machine makes. You can also ask each group to write down their sounds as if they were creating a musical score; this could serve as a memory aid. Groups can do the notation in notes, words, or symbols. Here is an example of what the score might look like if a group has four instruments and one member uses his voice:

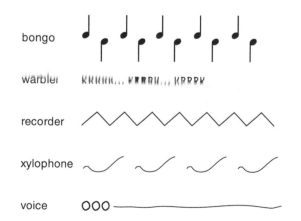

Allow the groups 5 to 20 minutes to prepare, then take turns performing this "mechanical" music.

Variation: Have the groups draw their own sound machines. Introduce movement into the game. If the groups are large enough, one half can make sounds and the other half the corresponding movements.

84

Musical Portrait

Requires: Many different instruments, index cards, blackboard and chalk or markers and an easel

Choose instruments with plenty of possibilities for expression. (Cymbals will not work here.) Then have everyone write her name on a card and write the name of an instrument below the name.

Collect the cards, shuffle and deal them. Everyone should have someone else's card. Using the instrument named on the card, and without any words, each person in turn has to try and let the group know whose name was on the card. Set a time limit of thirty seconds to a minute. If the group guesses correctly, the player may hand in her card. If not, she keeps the card and the game continues with the next person. In the following round the first player gets to try again.

Play is over when all the cards are handed back.

Variation: Instead of using the names of participants, use names of animals, countries, or professions. If you choose this variation, make a list of all the names on the board. Have everyone write a name on the card and the name of one of the instruments available below it.

85

Helping Out Song

Seat the group in a circle. Ask one person to think of a well-known song, and to sit in the middle of the circle and act out part of the song. As soon as someone else recognizes the song, he can try to help the first player out by adding to the improvisation. All of this must take place without anyone speaking. When nobody else "jumps in" to help, or everyone knows the name of the song, a new player introduces another song.

86

The Difficult Imitation

Requires: A CD or cassette player, a large room

Ask everyone except one person go out of the room. The person who stays should make up a rhythm, tune, or a series of sounds. Now call one group member back into the room and have the player present the piece. The player may stay in the room to watch as the second person presents the piece to a third person, who will then present it to a fourth person, and so on.

Record the entire sequence. Play it back at the end and note the difference between the first and final rendition of the piece. Where did the differences occur?

87

Moving a Round

Divide the players into two groups. Have them sing a well-known, two-part round such as "London Bridge Is Falling Down." Then have each group think of movements to go with the words. The simplest way is to make up different movements for each line.

Give them a short time to prepare, and then sing the round once to practice the movement. First try the song in two parts. If this goes well, have three or four groups work together.

88

On the Football Field

Divide the players into four or five smaller groups and give each group a number. Have each group choose a cheer or slogan related to football, such as "defense! defense!" or "touchdown!"

Place the groups in a row and stand in front of them. Now, when you hold up one hand with a certain number of fingers raised, the group with that number must repeat their phrase as loud as possible until you lower that hand. If you hold up the other with a different number of fingers raised, another group joins in with their cry. In this way you can recreate in a controlled way the atmosphere of a football field.

Seeking and Guessing Games

The games in this section are intended for children. At a certain age, children adore puzzles and riddles and enjoy testing each other. The games in this section allow you to connect with this particular developmental phase.

The primary objective is to help children discover and use musical material in a variety of ways. These games also teach children how to consider things from more than one angle and devise unusual solutions. At the same time, they strengthen imagination and intuition, two important aspects of creativity.

Chief Characteristics

- These games encourage individuals to look for a solution to a set problem.

- You can often make the games more exciting by introducing an element of competition.

- The looking and guessing usually require careful listening to recognize or track down something that is being played or imitated.

89

Which Sound Is This?

Requires: Many different kinds of instruments

Seat the group in a circle and place as many different instruments as possible in the middle. Each person then uses one of the instruments to imitate a sound. It may be a bird, such as a woodpecker, cuckoo, or canary; an animal, such as a horse or elephant; a household appliance, such as a vacuum cleaner or coffee grinder; motor vehicles; even other instruments. Begin the game by imitating something yourself. The person who guesses correctly takes the next turn, and so on. The game can go on in this way until no one can think of anything new or time runs out.

Note: It is essential to have several instruments available since the inspiration will come, to a large extent, from the possibilities inherent in the instruments. It may be helpful to let the group experiment with the instruments first.

90

What Am I?

Requires: Index cards with the names of instruments written on them, pins or sticky tape

Seat the group in a circle. Pin or tape on each person's back a card that has the name of an instrument written on it. No one knows what is on his back but everyone is allowed to look at their neighbors' cards.

The aim of the game is to have each person discover what is written on his card. The players form pairs, and the partners take turns asking each other questions that can only be answered with a yes or no. After each question it is the other person's turn. For example, one person can begin by asking "Is it a stringed instrument?" The partner answers yes or no, then asks her own question. This continues until one of them correctly guesses the instrument written on his card.

91

Which Song Is This?

Requires: Sheets of paper or cards with the first words of songs written on them

Divide the players into three or four small groups and seat the groups separately. Hold up a sheet of paper on which you have written—in large letters—a word or two from the opening of a well-known song. Everyone must be able to see the word at the same time. The first group to recognize and sing the song wins a point. Repeat this with different songs. The group that collects the most points is the winner.

Variation: Instead of words, use drawings to represent the situation in the song.

92

Looking for Instruments

Requires: A wooded area that is safe for play, enough instruments for half of the group

Divide the players into two groups. Each person in Group 1 takes a different instrument and finds a place to hide in the woods. Once they have found a good place, they stay there and keep playing their instruments. Group 2 gets a list of the instruments given to the first group and has to track them down in the order they appear on the list. Once they find an instrument they can cross it off the list, and the person playing that instrument gives them a word chosen at random.

When Group 2 has tracked down every instrument on the list, they make a sentence using all the random words they have collected and give the sentence to you. Make a note of the time it takes for Group 2 to find all the instruments and return with the sentence.

Now the groups change places and Group 1 gets to work, with a new list. The group that takes less time wins.

Variations: Players can complete the tasks individually, instead of working in a group. Give each person in Group 2 a separate list with the instruments in a different order. The first person to bring you a sentence is the winner from that group.

You can substitute songs for the instruments. The group members in hiding are given cards with the names of songs, and they have to keep singing their song until they are discovered.

93

Telephone Game

Requires: Dice, paper, pens, 14 players

Ask one person to leave the room. Have the other thirteen sit or stand in a circle and give them each a number starting from 0 to 12. Choose a song—or have the group choose one—and give the person who has the number 0 the starting note of the song. Assign the first 12 words of the song to the players number 1 to 12.

Now ask the person who left the room to return, and to throw the dice four times, twice with one die and twice with two. On a sheet of paper write the number 0, then the numbers that come up on the dice in the order they appear (for example, 0–2–5–11–7, the last two being the sum of the two dice). The person rolling the dice—the "caller"—should touch the people who have been given those numbers. The person with the number 0 sings her note and the others say their words. When the caller guesses the song correctly, another player takes her place and leaves the room. If she cannot work out the song, she has to "dial" a new number by rolling the dice again.

94

Guess the Proverb

Requires: Instruments, index cards with proverbs written on them

Seat the group in a circle and give each an index card with a proverb written on it. Have members of the group take turns choosing a key word from their proverb and making the sound that belongs to it, either with an instrument or with their voice. For instance, if a player's proverb is "don't count your chickens before they're hatched," he might make a chicken sound. The others have to guess the proverb. If they cannot guess, the person making the sounds has to choose another key word and give a sound to that. This continues until every proverb has been guessed.

Variation: Substitute a list of professions for the list of proverbs.

95

Musical Lucky Dip

Requires: Pictures from magazines, envelopes

Prepare ahead by cutting out pictures from magazines. These are used to depict a number of well-known songs. For example, use a picture of a clock for "Rock Around the Clock," a banjo for "O, Susannah." Cut out twelve pictures, put each in a separate envelope, and place all the envelopes in a box. Then, write a complete list of the songs on a board or a big sheet of paper.

Divide the players into three or four smaller groups. Each group takes a turn choosing an envelope from the box. They then have 30 seconds to guess the name of the song and to start singing it. If they get it right, they win a point; the team with the most points is the winner.

96

Draw Your Song

Requires: Blackboard and chalk or markers and an easel

Divide the players into three or four groups. Give the groups a short time to plan, then have a representative from each group go to the board and draw something from a well-known song (such as a jail window from "Jailhouse Rock," or a shoe from "Diamonds On the Soles of Her Shoes.") Have the other groups try to guess and sing the song. The first to do so correctly get a point. Group members do not have to wait until the drawing is finished.

When everyone from each group has had a chance to draw, count up the points and see which group wins.

97

Musical Secret Code

Requires: A blackboard and chalk or markers and an easel

Agree in advance on a musical code in which words can be translated into notes and vice versa. One way to do this is to assign each letter of the alphabet a note in the chromatic scale, beginning with middle C, as shown below.

The group can use this system to ask questions in musical notation. Answers can be given in the same way.

98

Letter Game

Requires: Sheets of paper, pens, newspaper

For this game, have members play individually or in small groups. Give each player or group a sheet of paper that is divided into three columns. Title the first column "instrument," the second "group," the third "song."

Have each person in turn choose a letter of the alphabet at random. One way to do this is to have them close their eyes and make a mark with a pencil on a page of the newspaper. The first letter the pencil marks is the one to use. Then give all the players one minute to fill in the different columns with as many instruments, groups, and songs they can think of that start with that letter.

When each person or group has had a chance to choose a letter, read all the papers aloud and count up the items on them. The person or group with the correct entries wins.

Musical Board Games

The board games in this section include a number of longer games in which the players throw dice to follow a course mapped out by the leader. You can play on a board or set up your own course in the room. Players must perform musical assignments at each stopping point.

Award a mark to each performance. The winner is the person who has the highest score at the end of the game.

These games could just as appropriately be in the section of games designed to enhance self-expression and improvisational skills. I have given them a section of their own because they require a longer time to play and have a specific form with their own possibilities of variation.

The fact that these games offer a completely fixed sequence of steps can provide, for children in particular, the incentive to be more adventurous in their individual performances. You can repeat this type of game often, provided that you vary the assignments.

Chief Characteristics:

- First, recognize that these games include all of the characteristics of games that help develop self-expression.

- As mentioned above, these games can be played on a board or live. If you use a board you can make up your own version and play with counters. If you play live, set up a whole room or part of a building as the course, with people or even groups acting as counters.

- In good weather, these games lend themselves to outdoor play. If you have access to a wooded area, for instance, you could work out a musical treasure hunt and perhaps define the route by musical code. (See Game 102.)

- Board games or treasure hunts like this can be worked out by the group members themselves (see Game 101). This helps stretch the imagination of group members and provides interesting experiences.

- A large number of people can easily take part in a live game set up in a room. This larger group can be subdivided into groups of three, four, or five who stay together during the game. The board versions can be played only by small groups. Otherwise, there is too much waiting involved.

- Allow time to prepare for this kind of game—and enough time to execute it. The pleasure to be gained from these games is ample compensation for the preparation and planning.

99

Live Board Game

Requires: Index cards with musical assignments written on them, instruments, dice, materials the play group will need to carry out your assignments

To Prepare

Plan a route that goes through the whole or part of the building. Decide the length of the route based on the time and space available. Make use of corridors, different rooms, the attic, the basement, etc. Mark the sequence with a string or provide written directions.

Be sure to number each room or point, since certain points along the route will have tasks assigned to them. You could, for example, leave a task at every other point along the route.

The assignments should be worded clearly, possibly humorously, and should test the creativity of the participants. Most of the game's excitement comes from these tasks. Each assignment represents a new challenge, and when you devise them you are building the excitement into the game. Set out everything the players need to carry out the assignments in advance—instructions, pens, paper, instruments, cassette recorders, etc.

The assignments do not always have to be done on the spot—the group can always be sent elsewhere, even outside, to complete a task. If you do this, however, be sure that all the necessary supplies will be available there.

Possible Assignments

1. Impersonate an instrument and play it.

2. Perform a monkey dance to the accompaniment of bongo drums.

3. Sing a song using just the sounds "hee-hee-hee" or "ha-ha-ha."

4. Sing three songs at the same time without laughing.

5. Pour water to different levels in five glasses so they will make different notes when tapped. Play a simple tune on the glasses.

6. As a group, impersonate a machine using sound and movement.

7. How many seconds can the group hold a note?

8. Make up a song with four lines about _____.

9. Sing a song using animal noises.

10. Make up a 30-second advertisement.

11. Note all the sounds you hear at this moment.

To Play

Divide the players into groups of three or four. Give each group a die and a check card, which can only be filled in by the organizers of the game.

The groups roll the die and move forward according to the number of points rolled. It is easiest if the groups start at five-minute intervals, instead of all at once.

Let members of the group know that what is important is *not* getting to the finishing line first but performing the assignments in the most original way they can. That is how they will gain points.

However, set a time limit for the assignments, otherwise the game will drag on too long. Ask the organizers to keep time. Only when an organizer has checked an assignment and awarded points for it may the group move on to the next task.

100

School Board Game

Requires: At least three full sets of dice

To Prepare

Arrange a space where you can number six different rooms or
playing areas. In each room, the players will complete a task.
If you can manage it, have a group leader in each room to assist
with the timing and completion of the tasks.

Draw six pictures of a schoolhouse. Cut each of the
pictures into four pieces, to make twenty-four puzzle pieces.
Put the pieces into a box, which you leave someplace central.

Determine the tasks. Choose several for each room, so that
groups will not have to repeat an assignment if a roll of the
dice brings them back in the same room.

Possible Assignments

1. Make up a song with four lines that expresses how you
   feel about homework.

2. Think of as many songs as possible in which a woman
   is the lead singer.

3. Make up a radio commercial (with sound) that plugs
   your favorite lunch food. Tape it.

4. As a group, make a concert of sounds you hear at a
   playground.

5. Arrange yourselves as if riding in a bus. Sing a suitable
   song.

6. Make up an interview with a student who has just finished an exam.

7. Indicate with a musical instrument how you usually feel getting up in the morning.

To Play

Put the players into groups of four or five and give each a single die. Have each group roll a die to determine which room to enter. Once a group is in a certain room, the members must complete a task assigned to that room.

If group members perform the task particularly well, allow them to take a piece from the puzzle box, and throw the dice again.

The number that comes up on the die is added to the number of the room they are in. If the two numbers add up to more than six, subtract six to determine the next room.

The group moves to that room and completes an assigned task there. If they do a good job, allow them to choose another puzzle piece.

The first group to piece together the schoolhouse symbol wins the game.

101

Musical Treasure Hunt

Requires: A blackboard and chalk or markers and an easel for the musical code; the other supplies you need are determined by the tasks you create for this game.

To Prepare

To create a musical treasure hunt, plot out the description of the route in musical notation. You will have to devise a code to do this. Here is one example:

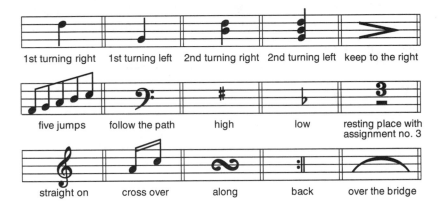

| 1st turning right | 1st turning left | 2nd turning right | 2nd turning left | keep to the right |

| five jumps | follow the path | high | low | resting place with assignment no. 3 |

| straight on | cross over | along | back | over the bridge |

You will also need to write down the assigned tasks on cards, and set out any necessary supplies in advance. Place the assignment slips at appropriate points along the route. (Alternately, you could post an organizer at each assignment point and make it her job to explain the assignment.) Certain assignments could be performed on the spot, others could be written down and performed—and in some cases judged—when everyone has come back together again.

Possible Assignments

Ideally, adapt the tasks to the surroundings. Here are a few examples:

1. Look for six different things—two animal, two mineral, two vegetable—you can whistle into.

2. Close your eyes for two minutes and write down all the sounds you usually hear in your classroom or at home.

3. Imitate a group of penguins playing in the water.

4. Form a rhythm group using anything you can find (such as sticks, stones, leaves, or your own body).

5. Use a tape recorder to record bird songs.

6. Sit on a bench and make up a song about what people usually do on benches.

7. Think of as many songs as you can about trees.

To Play

Divide the players into groups of three or four. Give each group a description of the route, a pen and paper, and send them off at regular intervals to follow the route. Apply some sort of points system to score the assignments yourself or by using the help of other organizers, and judge one group the winner.

101+

Board Game

20 Tell a joke.

19 Miss a turn.

18 Copy what your neighbour's doing.

21 In the well, wait until you are rescued.

22 Click your tongue 22 times.

37 Draw a musical instrument.

36 Dance like a gypsy with a tambourine.

35

38 Be as quiet as a mouse.

23 Keep your mouth closed for one minute.

39 Throw the dice and go back as many points as the number thrown.

40

24 Sing as high as you can.

25 Throw again.

26 Whistle a song on the kazoo.

27 Play a march on the drum.

START

1

2 Listen to the noises outside. Name three of the noises you can hear.

3 Buzz like a bee.

Sing like a canary.

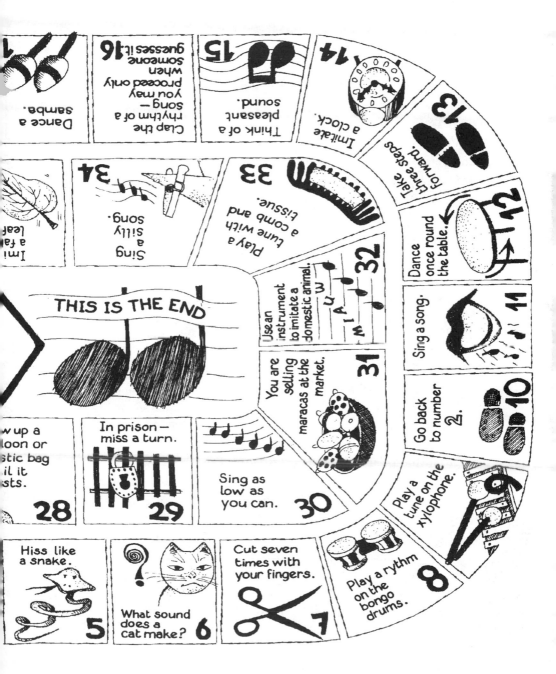

Index

SmartFun activity books encourage imagination, social interaction, and self-expression in children. Games are organized by the skills they develop and simple icons indicate appropriate age levels, times of play, and group size. Most games are noncompetitive and require no special skills or training. The series is widely used in homes, schools, day-care centers, clubs, and summer camps.

101 MUSIC GAMES FOR CHILDREN: Fun and Learning with Rhythm and Song *by* Jerry Storms

All you need to play these 101 music games are music tapes or CDs and simple instruments, many of which kids can have fun making from common household items. Many games are especially good for large group settings, such as birthday parties and day-care. Others are easily adapted to meet classroom needs. No musical knowledge is required.

Translated into 11 languages worldwide

160 pages ... 30 illus. ... Paperback $12.95 ... Spiral bound $17.95

101 MORE MUSIC GAMES FOR CHILDREN: New Fun and Learning with Rhythm and Song *by* Jerry Storms

This action-packed compendium offers musical activities which children play while developing a love for music. Besides listening, concentration, and expression games, this book includes rhythm games, relaxation games, card and board games, and musical projects. **A new multicultural section** includes songs and music from Mexico, Turkey, Surinam, Morocco and the Middle East.

176 pages ... 72 illus. ... Paperback $12.95 ... Spiral bound $17.95

101 DANCE GAMES FOR CHILDREN: Fun and Creativity with Movement *by* Paul Rooyackers

The games in this book combine movement and play in ways that encourage children to interact and express how they feel in creative fantasies and without words. They are organized into meeting and greeting games, cooperation games, story dances, party dances, "musical puzzles," dances with props, and more. No dance training or athletic skills are required.

160 pages ... 30 illus. ... Paperback $12.95 ... Spiral bound $17.95

For more information visit www.hunterhouse.com